JAZZ AGE FASHIONS

COLORING BOOK

MING-JU SUN

DOVER PUBLICATIONS, INC.
MINEOLA, NEW YORK

Spanning the 1920s, the Jazz Age was defined by opulence and flamboyance. Fashions of the time were no exception. In this gallery of Jazz Age fashion you'll find free-spirited women in short bobs, adorned in flowing dresses with sashes worn low on the waist. This style allowed these women (often dubbed "flappers") to more easily kick up their heels to popular dances of the time, such as the Charleston. Floral patterns were all the rage, as were pastel colors including Nile Green, French Blue, and Sunset Orange. Specially designed for the experienced colorist, the illustrations in this book will provide you with endless opportunities to experiment with color combinations and technique. Each of the thirty-one plates has been perforated for removal to make displaying your work easy.

Copyright

Copyright © 2017 by Ming-Ju Sun
All rights reserved.

Bibliographical Note

Jazz Age Fashions Coloring Book is a new work, first published
by Dover Publications, Inc., in 2017.

International Standard Book Number

ISBN-13: 978-0-486-81049-2
ISBN-10: 0-486-81049-6

Manufactured in the United States by LSC Communications
81049601   2017
www.doverpublications.com